Football

Football Made Easy

Beginner And Expert Strategies For Becoming A Better Football Player

By Ace McCloud

Disclaimer

The information provided in this book is designed to provide helpful information on the subjects discussed. This book is not meant to be used, nor should it be used, to diagnose or treat any medical condition. For diagnosis or treatment of any medical problem, consult your own physician. The publisher and author are not responsible for any specific health or allergy needs that may require medical supervision and are not liable for any damages or negative consequences from any treatment, action, application, or preparation, to any person reading or following the information in this book. Any references included are provided for informational purposes only. Readers should be aware that any websites or links listed in this book may change.

Table of Contents

DEDICATED TO THOSE WHO ARE PLAYING
THE GAME OF LIFE TO

KEEP ON PUSHING AND NEVER GIVE UP!

Ace McCloud

Be sure to check out my website for all my Books and Audio books.

www.AcesEbooks.com

Introduction

I want to thank you and congratulate you for buying the book, "Football: Football Made Easy: Beginner And Expert Strategies For Becoming A Better Football Player."

Football is a popular American sport that has been in existence since the late 1800s. Based on the sport of rugby, the object of the game is for two teams to bring the ball into their opponent's end zone to score points. The very first football game was played in New Jersey between two colleges, Rutgers and Princeton. The rules of the game were a mixture of rules from rugby and soccer. Since that first game in 1869, football has evolved into the popular sport we know today.

Today, football remains a very big deal in America. More than one million high schoolers play the sport each year, in addition to 70,000 college students and almost 1,700 professional players. Football is also popular among younger children, who are able to join recreational leagues. Many children who play when they are young remain involved throughout high school. Quite a few of those high school students go on to play in college.

Only a miniscule percentage of college players, those who are extraordinarily disciplined and dedicated, will end up playing on a professional team. The rest of the country's football lovers will continue to play on community leagues and in backyard pickup games. Many can be found in the stands or glued to their televisions, watching the games.

There are many benefits to playing football, no matter your age. Football can help you build discipline, commitment, strength, and a strong work ethic. Although football games are only played once weekly, most players practice at least five days a week to prepare. Football players of all levels must be committed to the game; this means they will drag themselves out to practice whether it is a hundred degrees outside or near freezing. This type of sport requires teamwork, which is great for building communication skills.

This book contains proven steps and strategies describing how to become a better football player, whether you are just starting out or you're well-experienced. In the next few pages, you will discover the basics of playing, the gear you will need, and you will learn some football terminology. Next, you will discover the best techniques for stretching and warming up, which can help your body maintain flexibility and decrease the risk of injury. Paired with that, you will discover the best secrets for nutrition and strength training. When done correctly, the right vitamins and minerals can transform you into a unstoppable athletic force!

The rest of the book covers the best strategies you can employ to improve your game, ranging from offensive and defensive strategies to strengthening your mental toughness. With football season just beginning, it's time to get your game on!

Chapter 1: Gearing Up

Knowing what kind of equipment you'll need for football is the first and most important step. The majority of sports require special equipment and football is no exception. Football equipment is divided into several categories: physical equipment used to play the game , apparel for team identification, protective gear for your body, and accessories and extras.

In any sport, safety is the number one priority. Knowing that you have the proper equipment and gear and familiarizing yourself with it before you even step onto the field is your first stride down the road to becoming a pro.

Obviously, the first thing you will need is the **football** itself, otherwise you have no game. You can buy a football almost anywhere – in most department stores and, of course, all sporting goods stores. Footballs come in all shapes in sizes, ranging from the soft brightly-colored and nearly weightless Nerf balls for kids all the way to industry-standard pigskins for teens and adults.

Serious athletes should use a ball with the specs dictated by the National Football League (NFL). According to the NFL, a football should be made of leather and will measure eleven inches long, slightly larger than footballs used for high school or recreational teams. The ball's circumference should measure twenty-two inches, should weigh fifteen ounces, and be pressurized at 12.5 pounds per square inch.

The **playing field** is equally important. According to the NFL, an official playing field should measure 120 yards long and 160 feet wide. Two white lines at each end of the field mark the end zones, which start with the goal line. End zones should stand ten yards deep.

The rest of the equipment you'll need is mostly for self-protection. Absolutely the most important gear you'll own is your **helmet**. Your helmet is designed to protect you from serious and potentially life-threatening injuries, which are all too common in football.

When choosing a helmet, the most important factors to consider are its size and its padding. A helmet that does not fit properly will not provide you with enough protection. To properly measure your head for a football helmet, wrap a tape measure around your head. Position it one inch above your eyebrows for the most accurate measurement.

You must also consider the padding of the helmet when you're fitting your head. There are two types of padding – air and foam. Air padding literally inflates with air, which may give your helmet the most accurate fit. Foam padding is simply pre-fitted padding made out of foam.

When choosing a helmet, you should also think about what position you will be playing, because helps to determine what type of facemask your helmet should have. There are two types of facemasks: open-caged and closed-caged. Open-caged masks provide players with an unobstructed view of the field. Players of skill, such as receivers, often wear open-caged masks.

Closed-caged facemasks differ because there is a vertical line running down the middle of the mask, sacrificing vision for extra protection. Closed-caged facemasks are better for defensive players and blockers.

Though open- and closed-caged masks are the two primary types, many manufacturers design facemasks to protect specific areas, such as the mouth, the eyes, or the nose. These specifications are generally marked with acronyms as follows:

OPO – Oral Protection Only

JOP – Jaw and Oral Protection

NOPO – Nose and Oral Protection Only

NJOP – Nose, Jaw, and Oral Protection

EGOP – Eyeglass and Oral Protection

Additionally, facemasks can come in a variety of styles and may include certain features, which are indicated by the following symbols:

R stands for reinforced, which means there is an additional bar beneath the one that originally comes over the top of the facemask. This helps to avoid stretching or warping of the opening.

DW stands for double wire, which adds an additional bar to the middle of the facemask; this also prevents stretching and warping.

SW stands for single wire, which is more common on open-face masks. Single-wire facemasks provide players with a better view, but with less protection.

UB stands for U-Bar, which is a u-shaped bar that sits over the bridge of the player's' nose. This bar can provide an open view of the field while also providing a great deal of protection.

Next, you'll want to consider the chinstrap for your helmet. Chin straps help keep the helmet attached firmly to your head and minimize its movement. Finally, you should look for the NOCSAE seal. NOCSAE stands for the "National Operation Committees on Standards for Athletic Equipment." This seal is a guarantee that you are buying a safe helmet.

You may also want to use a **neck roll** to provide additional protection to your head and neck. This roll, which is often made out of foam, is placed behind the neckline of your jersey. A neck roll can keep your head from snapping back; it also can help absorb the shock of any impact.

The second most important piece of safety equipment is your **shoulder pads.** Shoulder pads are important because football players tackle with their shoulders forward, exposing them to an increased risk of injury. Shoulder pads also help protect your ribs. Linemen in particular need stronger and more durable shoulder pads than players in other positions. Offensive players need light shoulder pads to allow greater freedom of motion. Shoulder pads come in many sizes. You can determine your size by measuring the width of your shoulders and your chest.

Your shoulder pads are covered by a **jersey**, which is a lightweight shirt made from a mixture of nylon and spandex. In football, the jersey represents the team for which you are playing. Official jerseys come with extra length to help you keep it tucked into your pants as well as a Velcro strip that attaches to another strip inside your pants. Optionally, you can tape the shoulders of your jersey to your shoulder pads. Depending on the team, your jersey may be a variety of colors and will usually bear a number, which helps spectators know who you are while you're on the field. Your jersey may also have your last name written on the back. For example, Eli Manning of The Giants wears a predominately blue jersey with his last name on the back, above his number, ten.

Gloves are important because they protect your hands and make it easier for you to catch and hold the ball. Receivers are known to wear **tact gloves**, which have a sticky rubber material in the palm. Linemen are known to wear gloves that have a thick padding, as their hands are more likely to get tangled in another player's mask or get crushed in a pile-up.

The gear you will wear below your waist depends on what position you play. All players wear tightly-fitted football **pants** which are made of nylon and spandex. They are designed with pockets designed to hold **knee and thigh pads**. The majority of players wear knee pads. Pads for your thighs are especially helpful for players who frequently come into physical contact with other players. Knee pads and thigh pads can be purchased as a package, which is a good option for somebody who plays a variety of positions. To wear these pads, you insert them into the pants before you put them on. **Hip pads** are designed to protect your pelvic area in the event of a hard fall. These are useful, because hip injuries account for approximately 10% of all injuries in football.

Football shoes are extremely important for protecting your feet and your knees. These shoes have spikes on the soles to give you traction in a variety of field conditions. Spikes range from ½ inch to 1 inch long. Companies such as

Nike and Reebok often manufacture football shoes and provide them to leagues in exchange for a contract.

Finally, there are some smaller and optional accessories that you can use to enhance your game.

All players should carry a squeezable **water bottle** to keep themselves hydrated throughout each game or practice. Since football is a highly active sport, it is easy for players to dehydrate quickly, even when the sun is not glaring down on the field. Dehydration can negatively affect both mental and physical abilities. If you frequently drink water, you can prevent overheating, fluid loss, and fainting from dehydration. If you prefer, you can substitute an electrolyte replacement beverage, such as Gatorade. Even if you don't feel thirsty, you should always drink at least a little when you have the chance. When active, be aware of and alert to the symptoms of dehydration, which include muscle cramps, fatigue, nausea, and lightheadedness.

A **first-aid kit** can also come in handy for games and practices. You can build your own kit by gathering the following: an icepack, adhesive bandages, antibacterial wipes, antibiotic cream, cotton swabs, hydrogen peroxide, athletic tape, an elastic wrap, gauze, extra padding, scissors, gloves, Vaseline, and tweezers. It can also be helpful to take a CPR class, just in case a teammate needs emergency help.

Positions and Players

If you're new to playing football, it is also important to become familiar with the different positions on each team. Traditionally, two teams play against each other on one field. When one team is playing on offense the opposing team will be playing defense. Eleven players must be on the field at all times, whether playing defense or offense

The offensive team possesses the ball. The aim of this team is to score points by getting the ball into their opponent's end zone. The offense breaks these players into two groups: One group consists of five **offensive linemen;** the other group consists of **backs and receivers**. The job of the linemen is to block the players on the other team while the backs and receivers work together to move the ball forward toward the end zone for a goal. Here are the different offensive positions:

Center – The center begins a play by passing the ball to the quarterback in an action known as "the snap." This player's location at the start of a play is in the center of the offensive lineup, hence the name. After the snap the center works to block opposing players. This player also calls out blocking assignments.

Quarterback – The quarterback is the player to whom the center passes the ball at the start of each play. At the start of a play, the quarterback is positioned directly behind the center. The quarterback is responsible for communicating each upcoming play to the rest of the offense. Following the snap, the quarterback can choose to run with the ball, to hand it off, or to pass it to another player.

Offensive Guard – The focus of the offensive guard is to protect the quarterback or offensive ball carriers. The two offensive guards are positioned on either side of the center.

Offensive Tackle – The offensive tackle seeks to block opposing players whose running and passing routes take them outside of the offensive guards' positions. The area between the two offensive tackles is known as the "close line of play" behind which clips from behind are allowed

Running Back – Running backs are players who run with the football. They are also known as wingbacks, tailbacks, or halfbacks.

Wide Receiver – Wide receivers are responsible for running to where they can catch the ball. These players are usually positioned "widely" on the field so they can easily run around the end of the defensive line and downfield near the sideline.

Tight End – Tight ends play alongside offensive tackles and share the responsibilities of both a receiver and an offensive lineman. They block the opposing team and are also available to catch passes.

Fullback – The fullback helps protect the quarterback at the start of play; he can also block for the running back.

The defense is the team that does not the ball. Their job is to defend their end zone and try to gain possession of the ball. Defensive players attempt to cause the offensive players to fumble (drop) the ball. They will also try to intercept a thrown ball, tackle a player who holds the ball, or otherwise prevent the other team from making progress toward their end zone. The defensive team often does not mandate specific positions for defensive players. However, there are some common positions that a defensive player might assume:

Defensive Tackle – Defensive tackles mainly defend against offensive ball-runners and often advance to put pressure on the quarterback.

Defensive End – The defensive ends are positioned on the outer ends of the lineup. Their primary function is to converge on the quarterback or other ball-carrier, either forcing him out of bounds or into the hands of other defenders.

Linebackers – Linebackers are positioned behind the main defensive line and are known as the heavy hitters of the defense.

Cornerback – The cornerbacks primarily block wide receivers. There are usually two cornerbacks playing at a time. Cornerbacks try to intercept the ball and rush offensive players.

Safety – Safeties are the team's last line of defense against runners and deep passes.

Chapter 2: Stretching And Warming Up

Although football players are best known for their power, strength, and size, being able to move effectively is a top priority if you want to be a pro.

As a football player, it is valuable to understand which muscles your body uses to perform at its best; this can help both your training and as you warm up. Warming up, which includes increasing your blood circulation and literally warming your muscles, is important to do before any high impact sport. Gradually ramping up your body's level of activity is less of a shock to your system and can prevent serious injuries from overtaxing unprepared body parts.

Stretching, after your body is warmed up but before you step into action, can help you move effectively and can increase your overall agility. Agility includes the ability to quickly change directions, a must in football. It is important to stretch each of muscle group, but your hips are key; the strength of your hip muscles is what allows you to make sudden stops, starts, and turns.

There are two types of stretches that are useful when preparing to play football: **static** and **dynamic** stretches. Static stretches are best to use after a training session or a game, because your body is already warmed up and the muscles are at their most flexible. Static stretches help improve your range of motion and increase your mobility. Dynamic stretches are better implemented prior to training or playing because they help reduce muscle stiffness.

Dynamic Stretches:

Arm Swings – Stand upright and hold your arms out to your sides, parallel to the floor. Slowly swing your arms together, scissoring them in front of your chest; then swing them back, stretching them slightly backward. Repeat this exercise for thirty seconds.

Trunk Rotations – Assume a normal standing position with your feet hip distance apart. Place your hands on your hips and slightly bend your knees. Keeping your feet flat on the ground at all times, slowly turn your head, neck and upper body as far as possible to the left. Then reverse the direction, with your torso following your head slowly all the way to the right. Repeat this motion a total of fifteen times

Hamstring Stretch – Lie on your back. Loop a towel around the bottom of one foot, holding the ends of the towel in your hands. Pull the towel to raise your leg until you feel a slight stretch along the back of the leg. Hold this for a few seconds, then gently lower your leg to the floor. Do this stretch ten times for each leg.

Toe Touches – Stand with your feet spread as far apart as possible. Stretch your right arm as far as you can toward your left toe. Stand back up and stretch your left arm as far as you can toward your right toe before rising again. Repeat this exercise ten times.

Side Stretches – Stand with your feet shoulder-distance apart. Keeping your chest straight, lean to one side. Avoid bending in either direction. Hold the stretch for two seconds and then repeat, leaning to the opposite side. Do this stretch for ten repetitions. As you are able, increase the number of sets.

Back Stretches – Lie on your back. Bend your knees and pull them to your chest. Fold your hands under the backs of your knees. Roll forward, allowing your feet to touch the floor. Then roll back until your head nearly touches the floor. Perform this stretch ten times.

Chest Stretch – Stand with your chest tall and your feet a little farther apart than your shoulders. Extend your arms straight forward with palms together. Keeping your arms straight, swing your palms apart until they are even with your shoulders, then reverse direction until you have returned them to the starting position. Continue this straight arm applause for ten times, increasing the speed as you go on.

For some visual examples of dynamic stretches, watch the YouTube video by Twin Cities Orthopedics entitled "Dynamic Stretching."

Static Stretches:

Static stretches are performed when your body is at rest. They are useful as a cool-down but can also be used to increase range of motion and flexibility by holding for thirty seconds.

Shoulder Stretch – Stand straight with your feet a little farther apart than your shoulders. Bend your knees slightly. Move your right arm forward, then swing the straight arm slowly inward across your chest, using your left arm to pull the upper arm toward your chest and feeling the stretch in your right shoulder. Hold the stretch for a few seconds and then release both arms. Repeat this stretch with the opposite arm.

Biceps Stretch – Stand straight with your feet slightly more than shoulder width apart. Keep your knees slightly bent. Hold your arms out so that they're perpendicular to the ground. Stretch your arms back as far as you can until you feel the stretch in your biceps.

Triceps Stretch – Stand straight with your feet slightly more than shoulder width apart. Keep your knees slightly bent. Stretch your right arm straight above your head and then bend your elbow, allowing the hand to fall behind your head. Reach your left arm over your head so that your hand can cup the right elbow, then pull back with your left hand until you feel the stretch in your right arm. Hold for ten to twenty seconds and release. Repeat this stretch for the left arm.

Upper Back Stretch – Stand straight with your feet slightly more than shoulder width apart. Keep your knees slightly bent. Cross your arms at the wrists and raise them above your head. You should feel your upper back begin to loosen up and stretch between your shoulders.

Calf Stretch – Position yourself so that you face a wall or another stable surface but are a step back from it. Step one foot forward and lean your hands against the wall, keeping your hands the same height as your shoulders. Keep the other leg straight as you allow your weight to press your heel to the ground. Feel the stretch in the calf of your back leg. Push yourself off the wall and then repeat, using the opposite leg.

Groin Stretch – Sit tall on the floor. Press the bottoms of your feet together. Gently hold your ankles and slowly press your knees toward the ground. Feel the stretch in your groin and thighs.

More Helpful Stretches for Athletes:

Quadriceps Stretch – Stand near a wall or use a chair for balance. Bend one leg behind you and use your free hand to hold your bent leg by the foot. Slowly pull up on your foot to feel the stretch in your thigh.

Arm Rotator Stretch – Stand and hold one arm up at a ninety-degree angle, as if you are going to wave at somebody. Grasp a broomstick vertically in your right hand and slip it behind your arm, grabbing the end in your right hand. Use your left hand to pull the bottom of the broomstick slightly forward and gently stretch your rotator. Repeat this stretch on the left side of your body.

Alternating RDL – Stand tall and keep your feet together. Bend forward, keeping your back straight until your back is parallel to the floor. Balancing on your right foot, raise your left leg behind you until it is also parallel to the floor. Extend your arms out sideways to help your balance. If necessary, put one hand on a chair to steady yourself. Lower your left leg as you rise to a standing position. Then, repeat this exercise on your left leg.

Lower Calf Stretch – Sit on the ground with your legs together. Keeping your body upright and straight, stretch your arms toward your feet as far as you can, feeling the stretch down the back of your leg. Hold for ten seconds and release.

Lying Knee Roll Stretch – Lie on your back with your arms straight out from your sides on the floor. Bend both knees and lower them together toward your left until they're on the ground. Allow your back and hips to stretch for a few seconds. Slowly return your bent legs to the upright position and then continue to the right to stretch that side in the same fashion. Repeat this exercise four times.

Groin Stretch – Sit on the floor and place the soles of your feet against each other so that your knees are pointing toward opposite walls. Sitting with a straight back, use your hands to push your knees toward the ground while you push your chest out to arch your back.

Reverse Lunge with Reach – Start with your feet hip distance apart. Take a large step backwards with your left leg, extending it straight as you lower your body, bending your right knee to a ninety degree angle. Be careful that your knee does not move forward beyond your toes.

As you lunge backward, raise your hands above your head. When your legs are firmly set, turn your torso to the right and stretch up and slightly forward with your arms. You should feel a pull from your left arm down your left side. Then, turn your upper body to face forward, lowering your arms as you pull your back leg forward, and rise to a standing position. Repeat the backward lunge, this time stepping back with your right leg.

Kneeling Hip Stretch – Kneel on your right leg, your left foot flat on the floor ahead of you and your left leg making a ninety-degree angle. Tuck your hips under to feel the stretch. Then relax and repeat, kneeling on the other leg.

Lower Back Stretch – Lie on your back. Pull each knee toward your chest while keeping your shoulders on the ground. Hold for a few seconds and release.

Hip Flexor – Get down on your right knee with your left foot firmly planted before you. Pull your right foot upwards so that the knee presses into the ground. Extend your left leg forward and stretch both hands toward your left foot. Repeat on your left knee.

Hip Flexor Stretch 1 – Get down on that right knee again and place your left foot on the ground before you, with the knee bent at a ninety degree angle. Slowly raise your arms as you press your hips forward. Stretch for a few seconds, then release. Repeat the process with the left knee.

Hip Flexor Stretch 2 – Stand on your right knee as before, but this time reach your right arm over your head to the left as you allow your hips to extend out to the right. Hold for a few seconds, then release. You'll repeat this exercise, standing on the left knee.

Hip Flexor Stretch 3 – Standing on your right knee as before, hold your arms out from your sides and slowly rotate your torso, first to the right, then to the left. Repeat the stretch, standing on your left knee.

Hip Adductor Stretch – Stand with feet hip distance apart. With your right leg, take a large step, lunging to the right and bending the right knee to activate a stretch in the left inner thigh. Rise up, returning your right foot to its original position Keep your torso erect and your back straight during this exercise. Repeat the lunge to the left. Complete four lunges to each side.

Chapter 3: Improving Your Football Skills

Always Wear Your Equipment

Protective gear can be bulky to wear, annoying to carry around and hard to get into, but you should never play without it! All it takes is one wrong move or one bad tackle to get injured. You can never predict the size and scope of an injury – you could incur just a sprain or become so injured that you'll never play football again. It's not worth the risk, which is already high by the sheer reality of playing football. Your number one rule should always be to wear your gear!

Establish a Balanced and Consistent Workout Routine

If you're already an established football player, odds are that you already have a workout routine you stick to. If you're just starting out however, there's no need to fear. So far, you've learned some great warm-up exercises and in a few chapters you'll learn about the best strength training exercises to help you become a successful football player.

Whether you have a workout routine right now or not, keep in mind that you should **stick consistently** to one that is good for you. Inconsistent or incomplete training can cause raise complications. For example, one side of your body may grow stronger than the other, leading to problems of imbalance. If some muscles groups are overlooked, you might not have the strength to make it through a whole game. Later on in this book, you will discover the top five best workout routines for football, so if you haven't already established one, you will soon have a ready-made workout routine you can adopt.

Strengthen Your Work Ethic

While it is true that some people seem to have a natural, inborn talent for playing football, your abilities can only develop when paired with a drive toward success. You may be the world's next Joe Namath, but without matching your talent with the same amount of hard work, you may very well go unnoticed. Professional football is a very competitive sport. Some players start playing in Pop Warner leagues as early of five years old, though the most important training takes place in high school. High school players who work hard enough to attract attention at conference and state games have the best odds of being recruited to a college team. Some players even hire personal trainers and coaches to help them advance to this level of play.

Pursue Goals, Both On And Off The Field

As with any venture, not just football, success is never just dropped into your lap. You can hire the world's best coach, but unless you take his advice and work hard, you will not see results. You must have sufficient inner drive, if you want to make it to the top. To fuel your inner drive, it helps to set goals and visualize each task you need to accomplish to reach your goal. Your goals serve as roadmaps to keep you on track. Without goals and strategies to reach them, you are likely to veer off course onto something less important but more easily reached.

To stay motivated in your daily life, set goals and review them multiple times each day. One highly effective tactic is to write your goals down on paper and put them in a prominent location. Display them somewhere you can easily see and review them, perhaps in your home gym or as the background on your cell phone.

When you write something down, you tend to retain it much longer. Take a few minutes right now to write down some goals, if you haven't already. Write your goals in the form of positive affirmations of completion. For example, if you want to be a football pro, you might say, "I will easily train to become the world's next pro football player." Ensure that your goals and your "whys" for achieving them are as clear as possible. Write your vision in a compelling and exciting voice. Don't be afraid to dream big and shoot for something truly remarkable. Who says you *can't* make it to the NFL?

Visualize Your Success

Visualization can be powerful fuel for your motivation. Think about *what* you want and *why* you want it. Then, imagine what your life will be like once you've got it. For example, if you are working hard as a college football player, think about what your life will look like after you've signed your first deal as a professional player. Will you drive an expensive car and living in a mansion? Envision the lifestyle and the relationships that are important to you.

Visualization is something the top pros in the world do on a consistent basis. Make visualization a habit, something you do every day. This will dramatically increase your chances of success. You can also visualize a scene as if you were ten to fifteen feet away in the third person. Just allow the scene to progress naturally as you perform each task perfectly to reach your desired objective.

Run Every Day

Cardiovascular exercise, especially running, can help your body maintain peak performance. You should make it a practice to run at least three miles every day. Run uphill as much as possible and then walk back down once you've reached the top. Doing this every day can help you remain strong and fit so that when you're on the field, running won't take all your attention and effort.

Practice Speed Exercises

Speed is an important factor in football. The ability to maintain a fast speed is important for your success. You can do this by consistently practicing speed exercises. Speed is not an inborn talent nor does it develop overnight. You must develop speed over time. In football, speed is broken down into two aspects: **stride rate** and **stride length**. Stride rate is the speed at which your arms and legs cycle when you sprint. Stride length is the amount of ground you can cover between strides. When you combine stride rate and stride length you can increase the amount of ground you can cover, which is important if you want to outrun your opponents and reach their end zone with the ball.

Exercise 1 – Stride Rate Development – Arms

Stand in front of a mirror, feet shoulder-width apart. Stand tall and quickly pump your arms in a sprinting motion as fast as you can for twenty seconds. Take a one-minute rest period; then repeat the process four more times. When you feel you've mastered the twenty second interval, increase it to thirty seconds.

Exercise 2 – Stride Rate Development – Feet

Stand in front of a mirror, feet shoulder-width apart. Bend your arms as if preparing to sprint. On command, run in place as quickly as possible. Do this five times for twenty seconds each, with a one-minute rest period in between.

Exercise 3 – Stride Length Development – Knees

Stand in front of a mirror, feet aligned with your shoulders. Flex your arms as if preparing to sprint. On command, run in place as quickly as possible, bringing your knees up to hip-height.. Do for this five times in twenty-second intervals with a one minute rest period in between.

Exercise 4 – Stride Length Development – Squats

Squats help build the muscles you need to support your speed development. Stand with your feet shoulder-width apart. Keep your head up and squat down. Your knees should not extend forward beyond your toes and your butt should be as low as your knees. Perform this exercise in five sets of twenty repetitions each.

Exercise 5 – Stride Rate and Stride Length Development – Sprints

Whenever you plan to run sprints, be careful to warm up your muscles first. Find an open area such as a field, where you can run up to fifty yards in a straight line. The objective of this exercise is to combine everything you have practiced in the previous four exercises Begin with running five sprints with a three minute rest period in between. Over time, work up to a total of ten sprints in a single setting. At the end of this workout, take your time to let your heart rate decrease and perform some gentle stretches while your body is still warmed up and limber.

Work on Your Passing Routes

Are you familiar with those diagrams with circles and arrows, flying all over a drawing of a playing field? Those diagrams represent passing concepts and route combinations for players. Since receivers, running backs, tight ends and other players are prevented by their opponents from running in a straight line, it is important to familiarize yourself with various passing routes designed to help you lead your team to victory. There are at least thirty different types of passing routes. The most common are:

The Angle – This route is for halfbacks and fullbacks who run in the backfield or provide zone coverage. You run toward the outside of the field of players, then you angle back toward the center. As long as you are faster than the player who is defending you, this route can be very effective.

The Bubble – This route works best for receivers. A receiver will step backwards and make a horizontal run. He must stay focused on the quarterback, who is waiting to throw him the ball. The receiver catches the ball and then begins to hotfoot it up-field.

The Corner – This route works best for receivers who play with cornerbacks that are positioned in the flat zone area. The receiver runs straight downfield and works his way to the end zone corner.

The Curl – This route works well for receivers who work man-to-man and zone coverage. In this play, the receiver runs in a straight line up the field and then curls back toward the quarterback. If the throw is timed right, this route allows the receiver to make a leaping catch.

The Deep Cross – This route is best for receivers who play man-to-man coverage and works best when you are faster than your defenders. You will run twelve yards across the field and well behind the line of scrimmage, angling forward at one point toward the sideline.

The Deep Comeback – This route is best for receivers who play against soft zone coverage. In this route, the receiver runs twenty yards downfield and then hooks toward the quarterback.

The Deep In – This route is best for receivers who play against underneath coverage. In this route, the receiver runs ten yards downfield and then suddenly moves to the middle of the field.

The Deep Out – This route works best for receivers who play soft zone coverage. The receiver moves ten yards downfield and then moves in a ninety-degree angle toward the sidelines.

The Delay – For this route to work, the running back must lag before acting out on his route. The lag makes it appear to the other team that he is pass-blocking.

When performed correctly, the delay can be powerfully effective against both man-to-man and zone coverage.

The Dig – This route is great for receivers. The receiver moves downfield and then makes a sudden move into the middle.

The Fade – This route is good for receivers and can work well against the bump-n-run. The receiver will take an outside release to avoid the quarterback and then perform a touch-pass.

The Flat – In this route, the receiver runs the area outside the hash marks in the field and up to ten yards ahead of the line of scrimmage. This route is good for man-to-man coverage, provided the receiver can run faster than the defense.

The Go – In this route, receivers run straight upfield and fade toward the sideline when they reach the end of the route.

The Hitch – In this route, the receiver runs down field for a few steps before stopping and looking toward the quarterback for a pass.

The In-n-Up – This route makes it look as if the receiver is running an in route until he breaks upfield. If the other team comes in to defend, the receiver can throw the ball as he is breaking.

The Option – With the option, the receiver can run one of two possible routes, depending on what he thinks is best based on the pass coverage. Since the receiver does not always choose the best route, this is not as popular.

The Out-n-Up – The receiver runs and breaks toward the sideline before quickly breaking toward the field.

The Post – In this route, the receiver runs fifteen yards downfield before cutting to the center and running toward the goalposts.

The Quick Out – The receiver runs downfield for five straight yards and then makes a sudden ninety-degree movement toward the sidelines.

The Shallow Cross – The receiver runs straight for five yards and then suddenly moves into the middle, looking to catch the ball.

The Shake – This route is best for receivers who play defense. In this play, the receiver makes several sudden moves and then ultimately heads toward the middle of the field. The sudden cuts allow him to get away from any defensive players that are covering him.

The Slant – In this route, the receiver runs downfield in a straight line for five yards and then slants at a forty-five-degree angle. If the timing is right on this route, it can be extremely powerful and almost unbreakable.

The Smash – The receiver runs in a "Z" shape toward the sideline, cutting in and out of the middle of the field.

The Spot – In this route, the receiver starts out running the slant but then hooks back to the quarterback near the line of scrimmage. The ball should be thrown before the receiver hooks toward the quarterback.

The Streak – The receiver runs downfield as quickly as possible, away from the cornerback.

The Stick – In this route, the receiver runs four yards upfield and heads toward the quarterback.

The Stop-n-Go – In this route, the receiver runs downfield for seven yards; then he will pause and turn back toward the quarterback. The receiver will turn around again and continue running in a straight line upfield.

The Swing – This route is good for running backs. The running back heads out at a ninety-degree angle before rounding his way up the field. This route works well if the running back is faster than his opposing player.

The Whip – This route is best for receivers. The receiver runs a quick inside route and then stops and pivots toward the sidelines.

The Wheel – The receiver rounds out to the sideline and then breaks upfield. This pass route is effective against zone coverage.

Offensive Strategies

The Wildcat Formation – The Wildcat formation works well when the shifting of skill players on one side becomes a mismatch. In this formation, the team replaces the quarterback with a running back who receives the ball from the center at the snap. The running back can choose to pass the ball to the "man in motion," throw the ball to someone else or run with the ball himself. The Wildcat formation makes it difficult for the opposing team to defend because it creates confusion.

The West Coast Offense – The West Coast Offense is a strategy that enables the team to control the ball with the help of a short passing game. The purpose of this strategy is to get the linebackers and safeties away from the line of scrimmage by utilizing quick and horizontal passing routes from a horizontal approach. The West Coast Offense overwhelms the opposing team with receivers.

The Shotgun Formation – In The shotgun formation, the quarterback is positioned about five yards behind the center at the start of a play. The advantage of this formation is that it enables the quarterback to throw the ball as soon as he receives it.

The Pistol Formation – The pistol formation is initially set up like the shotgun formation, except the quarterback is positioned only three yards behind the center and has a running back behind him. The advantage of the pistol formation is that it gives the offensive team more options when the ball is passed to the quarterback.

Defensive Strategies

Gap Control

The area between two offensive linemen is known as a "gap." These gaps are broken down into four groups. The "A" gap is the area between the center and the guard. The "B" gap is the area between the guard and the tackle. The "C" gap is between the tackle and the tight end and the "D" gap is the area outside of the tight end. The purpose of gap control or gap defense is to make sure that the defensive players have each offensive gap covered. When planned right, gap control can enable a defender to get past a lineman.

Many coaches use a system to correctly line up each defender before the start of a play. While the system is not standardized, what I describe below will provide a basic understanding of how the numbering system works.

Position 0 means a player stands head-to-head facing the center.

Positions 2, 5, and 8 mean that the player is standing head-on, facing a guard, a tackle, or an end, respectively.

Positions 1, 4, and 7 mean that the player is aligned to the inside of a guard, a tackle, or an end, respectively. "Inside" refers to the shoulder of the opponent that is closer to the center of the field.

Positions 3, 6, and 9 mean the player is aligned to the outside of a guard, a tackle, or an end, respectively "Outside" refers to the opponent's shoulder that points toward the sideline.

Learn From The Professionals

Sometimes the best way to learn is to model yourself after a professional player. Some youth players have the privilege of attending football camps where professional players will come and help players improve their skills. If you are an older player, you can still learn this way, even if you are not physically interacting with a pro. You can pick a player you admire the most and do several things to obtain information about him. You can read about your mentor to learn what brought them into the pros. You can watch your model play and imitate his strategies. You can emulate his training routine, his mental strength, and his outlook on the game.

Help Your Body Heal

Even if you don't suffer major injuries on the field, it is important to help your body heal and recover during the off-season. Most athletes will have muscle imbalances or issues with joint alignment. Left untreated, small issues like these can develop into serious chronic problems when you're training later on. One way to combat these issues is to focus on recovering your soft tissue, utilizing foam rolling, stretching. It is equally necessary to use the off-season to work on keeping your joints healthy.

Practice Yoga During The Off-Season

Yoga can help you improve your functional range of motion during the off-season as well as strengthening your body to minimize the chance of injury. Here are some key yoga poses:

The Bridge – Strengthens spine muscles while improving posture

Lie on the floor with your feet flat, bending your knees at a ninety-degree angle with your heels tucked in. As you exhale, press your feet into the floor and raise your hips until your body is straight. Hold for thirty seconds before lowing your hips to the floor.

The Pigeon – Stretches thighs, hip flexor and back

Start by standing on your hands and knees. Keeping your hips square, pull your left leg forward, placing your left knee on the ground just behind your left hand. Swing your left foot to just behind your right hand. Lower both hips to the ground as you stretch your right leg behind you. Inhale as you push up with your arms. Exhale as you relax your arms.

The Cobra – Strengthens your spine

Lie on the floor with your legs out and your feet resting on the floor. Align your hands on the floor with your shoulders. Keeping your elbows tight, breathe out and straighten your arms so that your chest lifts off the ground. Do not let your shoulders point toward your ears. Instead, keep them down. Stay in this position for thirty-five seconds.

The Dolphin – Strengthens your shoulders, hamstrings, upper back and calves for increased mobility

Position yourself on your hands and legs. Put your forearms on the ground. Press your palms together and push your knees up from the floor. At the same time, raise your hips up as you press your arms into the ground. Hold this position for thirty-five seconds.

Practice Footwork Drills

Successful football players can accurately move around the field with speed, accuracy, and coordination. Practicing footwork drills can help you achieve this. These drills are important for all players, whether you are an offensive lineman or a defensive running back. Working on your footwork can help you find open spots on the field and may allow you to break through players. Here are some simple and easy footwork drills you can use to improve your performance:

Drill #1 – Tire Flips

Perform this drill in four repetitions, each rep lasting thirty seconds, with a 60 second rest in between. This drill helps improve footwork and can supplement any strength training program.

This drill requires the use of a large tire (ranging from 200 to 300 pounds). Reach down to grab the tire as you bend at your hips and knees. Driving through these joints, flip the tire forward, jump into the center and then jump out. Turn around so that you're facing the tire and flip it back. Complete as many flips you can in thirty seconds.

Drill #2 – Hexagons

Perform this drill in three repetitions of thirty seconds each, giving yourself a thirty-second rest period between repetitions. This drill can help improve your response to a sudden change of direction on the field.

Using tape or chalk, mark out hexagons on the field that measure one foot square across. Begin by standing in the middle of the tape or chalk. Quickly jump over the front of the marker and then jump back inside. Jump again, this time diagonally over the line. Jump back to the middle. Alternate jumps in a clockwise manner around the sides of the hexagon; then reverse your direction. Complete as many revolutions as you can in the space of forty seconds.

Drill #3 – Diamonds

Perform this drill in three repetitions of thirty seconds each, with a thirty-second rest in between. This drill utilizes a resistance band and can help you improve changing direction against resistance.

Using cones, create a diamond shape on the field, placing the cones six yards apart. Position yourself at the first cone. Pulling against the resistance, sprint toward any other cone and then back toward the first cone. Sprint back and forth between as many cones you can in thirty seconds.

Work On Hand-Eye Coordination – Hand-eye coordination is an important skill for football players, especially wide receivers. This skill enables you to use both hands and both eyes together to catch the ball. Hand-eye coordination is simple to practice:

Wall Ball – Using a rubber bouncy ball, find a tall, hard wall; throw the ball against the wall and practice catching it with one hand only. Once you have mastered catching it this way you can begin to throw it harder and harder, to improve your response time.

Five Yard Turns – Have a player stand five yards behind the quarterback, The quarterback will yell "hike" and pass the ball. The aim is for the other player to focus on just catching the ball without taking time to think about it. This drill not only helps improve hand-eye coordination, it also improves reaction time.

Reaction Ball Drill – A reaction ball is a ball that is extra bouncy and erratic. Two players should stand together while one of them bounces the ball. The other player's ambition is to catch the ball before it bounces for the second time. This type of ball helps improve agility and reaction time.

Practice Throwing Drills

There is much more to properly throwing a football than stretching your arm back and letting it fly. A proper throw requires the correct footwork and positioning on the field. Throwing drills are especially important for quarterbacks, who must learn to be fast *and* accurate. Here are some great throwing drills you can try:

The Two Knee Drill – The quarterback and a receiver kneel facing each other while ten yards apart. The receiver then holds his arms up and the quarterback throws the ball through his arms while kneeling. This drill enables the quarterback to focus on accuracy.

Footwork Throwing Drill – Place six cones along a yard line on the field, spaced two feet apart. The quarterback stands where the cones end, holding the ball, and facing downfield. The quarterback should begin by shuffling forward, shuffling backward, and then shuffling around each cone. When he hears "throw," he should stop and throw the ball to a receiver downfield. The coach should yell "throw" at different times.

Running Throws – Have the quarterback stand fifteen yards from another player. The quarterback should run about five yards and throw the ball to the partner, ensuring that his non-throwing shoulder points toward the receiver.

Chapter 4: Best Strength Training Programs

Strength Training

Strength training is important for football because it requires the intense use of your muscles. As you age, your muscle mass will naturally decline. However, keeping your muscles strong is important for burning fat, keeping your bones strong, boosting your stamina, managing chronic conditions, and it can even help keep you focused. As you build up your muscles, your body will be able to burn more fat and your bones can become strengthened, warding off osteoporosis, fractures, and sprains. Strength training can help you stay young as you get old and it can help reduce the risk of heart disease and diabetes.

While non-athletic bodybuilders often find it beneficial to pursue a routine approach to strength training, football requires specific types of strength training exercises at different times of the year. Your regimen may also vary, depending on which position you play. Linemen need bulk, body weight, and power. Wide receivers, tailbacks, and defensive backs need to build strength and power while maintaining speed and agility.

Your strength training program should consist of a cycle that changes throughout the year. In the off-season, you should spend as much time as you can on strength training. Your objective during the off-season should be to maximize your strength, size, and power. During the playing season, you should spend almost as much time on your muscles, but the intensity and volume of your regime should be reduced. During the transition between off-season and playing season, your objective should be to rest, recharge, and recuperate.

Though the strength training for each player will differ, it is important to include a period of **anatomical adaptation training** as part of your regime. This type of training can help balance all your muscles instead of lopsidedly focusing some and neglecting others. Beginning athletes should spend at least eight weeks in anatomical adaptation training, while more experienced trainers may only need three or four weeks. Anatomical adaptation training will balance your strength across your body and will prepare your tendons, ligaments, and connective tissues for the more intense and demanding parts of training.

Circuit Training

Circuit training is designed to build muscle. It combines a mixture of high intensity exercises with resting times to build the strength and endurance of your muscles. While circuit training can be highly effective, overwork can result in fatigue-related injuries which if not addressed may become chronic. Therefore, I recommend this as a focus for beginning your workout in the off-season.

Whenever you are building muscle, you are in essence tearing muscle fibers. Those tears need time to heal and grow, so any circuit training should be alternated with forty-eight hours of down time.

Here is one effective circuit training schedule:

Monday & Thursday:

Perform three sets of ten repetitions for each of the following:

Push Press – This exercises your shoulders and triceps, as well as engaging your hamstrings, glutes, and quadriceps. Using a weight rack, start by holding the bar on your chest, gripping it with your hands at shoulder width. Use the weight from your legs and arms to push the bar straight up over your head and lock it in place. Then lower the bar to its original position against your chest. Keep your back straight during this exercise. To check out the push press in action, go to YouTube and search for "Strength Camp eCoach: Push Press."

Hammer Curl – Hold a dumbbell in each hand and place your feet hip width apart. With your elbows staying barely ahead of your hips, curl both arms toward your chest as far as you can, exhaling in the process. To view the hammer curl, visit YouTube and search for "How To: Dumbbell Hammer Curl" by ScottHermanFitness.

Power Shrugs – Using a weight rack, position your hands at shoulder width and hold the bar with an overhand grip. Keeping your elbows completely straight and your arms hanging down, lift your shoulders straight up toward your ears, no rolling. Hold for about three seconds, and then release your shoulders. This exercise strengthens your trapezius muscles. For visual instructions, go to YouTube and watch the video by Matty Fusaro entitled "How to Perform Shrugs the Right Way for Traps."

Sumo Squats – Pick up the bar behind your neck and hold it throughout this exercise. Stand with your feet wide apart and pointing outward about forty-five degrees. Your weight should be mostly on your heels and the outer part of your feet. Keeping your eyes ahead and your straight back slightly bent forward for balance, lower yourself as if to sit down. Keep your hips well behind as you squat down until your thighs are parallel to the floor. Hold for a couple seconds, then return to your starting position.

Tuesday & Saturday:

Perform up to three sets of ten repetitions for each of the following:

Straight Leg Dead Lift – With your palms facing your body, hold a kettleball with both hands and stand straight with your knees slightly bent. Keeping your head facing forward and your back straight, bend forward from your waist until your back is parallel to the floor. Return to your starting position.

Forward Lunge – Stand with your feet shoulder width apart and hold a kettleball with both hands near your hips. Step your right leg forward, bending your knee until your thigh is parallel to the ground. Slowly lean forward and place the kettleball to the side of your forward leg. Return to your starting position and do the same with your other leg.

Upright Barbell Row – Position your hands on a bar, keeping them a little less than shoulder width apart, with an overhand grip. Rest the bar on top of your thighs and flex your elbows. Keeping your back straight, exhale and lift the bar using the sides of your shoulders. Make sure the bar stays close to your body, while you bring the bar up to your chin. Hold it, and then slowly lower the barbell as you inhale.

Chin-Ups – Keeping your hands close together, grasp a chin-up bar with an underhand grip so that your fingers are facing you. Stick your chest out and keep it straight as you curve forward the small of your back. Exhale as you pull your body up until your chin is over the bar. Squeeze your biceps before inhaling as you lower your body to the starting point.

Hypertrophy Strength Training

Hypertrophy strength training involves building the size and bulk of your muscles. Football players can benefit from large muscle mass for several reasons. First, larger muscles mean greater strength. Second, the heavier bulk gives you greater force when pushing. Hypertrophy strength training is safe, although – because of the intensity of the training – you are advised to proceed cautiously. This type of training should always be followed up with a series of functional strength training exercises in order to give your muscles opportunity to rebalance themselves.

Hypertrophy training generally lasts from four to six weeks with two to four sessions per week. The training usually consists of six to nine exercises with three to six sets and six to twelve repetitions per set. As with weight training, you should take a rest period of at least forty-eight hours between sessions.

What follows is a sample hypertrophy training routine that I highly recommend:

Monday, Wednesday, & Friday:

Stiff-Legged Barbell Deadlifts – This lift serves to strengthen your hamstrings. Stand with your feet hip-width apart. Bend at the waist – keeping your back straight and your head up – to grasp the barbell using an overhand grip with your palms facing the floor. Lift the barbell until you are standing straight up with knees slightly bent. This is your starting position.

Keeping your back flat and your eyes straight ahead, inhale as you bend your torso forward at your hips until you can feel the stretch in your hamstrings. As the barbell pulls your arms straight down, do <u>not</u> allow your shoulders to roll forward. After a couple seconds, exhale as you raise your torso – keeping your back straight and your eyes fixed on the far wall – until you have returned to your starting position.

Perform two sets of up to ten repetitions:

Dips – Find or make two stable surfaces slightly more than shoulder width apart. Suspend your body on your straight arms from these two surfaces, with your fingers pointing forward, bending your lower legs until you are hanging above the floor. Inhale as you bend your arms at the elbows and gently lower yourself, bending your arms less than ninety degrees. When you feel a stretch across your chest, exhale as you raise your body back up. If you are unable to raise yourself completely at first, it is okay to help yourself with your feet. Over time, you will be able to raise yourself back up with less assistance and then none at all.

Perform two sets of up to ten repetitions:

Dumbbell Cable Rows – The dumbbell method works the same upper body muscles as the rowing machine. Hold a dumbbell in each hand, with your palms toward your sides. Stand with your feet firmly planted, hip distance apart and your knees slightly flexed. Keeping your back flat, your shoulders back, and your head straight, bend forward at the hips until your back is almost parallel to the floor. Allow the dumbbells to keep your arms pointing straight downwards with the elbow barely flexed. This is the starting position.

Keeping your back and shoulders stable, breathe out as you pull the dumbbells straight up toward your body until they touch your sides. Hold briefly, then inhale as you slowly lower your arms to the starting position.

Perform one set of up to ten repetitions:

Dumbbell Shrugs – Stand tall and stationary as you hold a dumbbell in each hand with your palms to your sides. Exhale as you raise your shoulders straight up without rolling them. At the top of your shrug, hold for a few seconds, then, Slowly return your arms to your sides.

Perform one set of up to ten repetitions:

Seated Dumbbell Press – This exercise strengthens your shoulder muscles. Sit on a bench with your back against a support and pick up a dumbbell in each hand, resting them vertically atop your thighs. Use your thighs to help you bend your arms and raise one dumbbell at a time to shoulder height, rotating your arm until your palm faces toward you. This is your starting position.

Exhale as you push both dumbbells up until your arms are straight above your head and the dumbbells are touching. Hold this for a couple seconds, then lower the dumbbells back to the starting position as you inhale.

Perform up to two sets of ten repetitions:

Dumbbell Bicep Curls – Stand with your legs shoulder width apart, arms hanging down and holding a dumbbell in each hand. Without moving your triceps, breathe out as you use your bicep muscles to bend your arms at the elbows and curl the dumbbells. Once your arms are fully contracted, hold the position for a few seconds, tightening the muscles in your biceps. Inhale and gently return to your starting position.

Perform up to two sets of ten repetitions:

Crunches – Lie on your back and rest your feet flat on the ground. Place your left hand behind your head on your right shoulder. Put your right hand behind the left arm to touch your left shoulder. This will stabilize your neck and head, which should remain relaxed and at rest throughout this exercise.

From this starting position, inhale slowly. Exhale as you use your abdominal muscles to raise your shoulders off the floor. When your shoulders are four inches above the ground, hold this position for about five seconds, then relax to the starting position.

Perform from one to five sets of ten repetitions.

Maximal Strength Training

Hypertrophy training enables you to build strength by increasing the cross-sectional area of your muscles. However, that type of training does not allow your body to tune into your fast twitch motor units, which can provide you with quick response time. Maximal strength training often lasts between three to nine weeks, with four sessions per week. For the best results, it is recommended that you engage in hypertrophy training before you attempt maximal strength training.

Here is an effective maximal strength training routine:

Monday & Thursday:

Half Squats – Position a barbell on your shoulders as you keep your feet shoulder-width apart. Squat only halfway down (as opposed to a full squat) and lift the barbell up.

Perform up to three sets of eight repetitions.

Bench Presses – This exercise requires a racked bench. Raise your arms but do not lock them. Lift the bar and hold it above you. Exhale and push the bar away from your body. Return the bar to the rack.

Perform up to three sets of eight repetitions.

Seated Dumbbell Press – Sit on a utility bench with back support. Gripping two dumbbells, hold them so that your palms are facing forward. Use your thighs to position each dumbbell at shoulder height. Exhale and push the dumbbells until they make it to the top. Hold for a few seconds and then gently return to your starting position.

Perform up to three sets of eight repetitions.

Crunches – Lie flat on the floor with your feet on the ground. Hold your hands on both sides of your head, keeping your elbows tucked in. Bring your shoulders off the floor by pushing your lower back into the floor. Exhale as you bring your chest up. Hold the position when your shoulders are four inches off the ground, squeeze your abdomen muscles and then come back down to the ground.

Tuesday & Saturday:

Hang Cleans – Stand with your feet shoulder width apart and your weight on your heels. Grasp a bar in an overhand grip and let it hang down in front of you. Keeping your back straight, your knees flexed and your eyes on the far wall, bend at the hips until the bar is touching your kneecaps. This is your starting position. You should feel your hamstrings stretching.

Keeping your weight on your heels, your back straight and your knees flexed in a quarter squat, raise your upper body and pull your shoulders back until the bar is positioned on your upper thighs.

With great force, drive the weight of the bar upward through your hips and knees as you shrug the bar up to the top of your shoulders, then flex your knees and hips again until you are back in a quarter squat.

Return the bar to the starting position and repeat, performing up to three sets of eight repetitions.

Deadlifts – Grasp a dumbbell in each hand in an overhand grip; stand erect with your knees slightly bent and your arms hanging straight down in front of your upper thighs. This is your starting position.

Keeping your back straight and your shoulders steady, slowly flex your upper body forward at the hips, allowing the weights to pull your arms straight down. Continue the forward motion until your back is almost parallel to the floor, then reverse direction and slowly raise your torso until you have returned to the starting position.

Repeat this motion for up to three sets of eight repetitions.

Lat Pull Downs – Stand with your feet slightly apart, your shoulders back, and a dumbbell in each hand in an overhand grip, as before. Keeping your back straight and your shoulders steady, slowly flex your upper body forward at the hips, allowing the weights to pull your arms straight down until your back is parallel to the floor. The backs of your hands should be pointing forward. This is your starting position.

Stay in this position as you slowly pull your arms straight backwards until they are at your sides, parallel to the floor. Then, slowly return them to the starting position.

Perform up to three sets of eight repetitions.

Power Training

Power training is what helps athletes transform their strength into movements that are specific to football by enabling their muscles to rapidly contract. Since circuit, hypertrophy, and maximal strength training do not provide this type of strength to your muscles, power training should be the final phase of your workout. Power training is relatively complex and is broken down into three different types:

Pylometrics – Pylometrics utilizes light loads and fast movements as your contractions become less eccentric. The only downside of pylometrics is that the exercises can lead to wear and tear injuries.

Ballistics – This form of power training utilizes light loads such as in pylometrics. The big difference is that this form applies force through a full range of motion.

Isotonic Weight Lifting – This form of power training utilizes traditional strength training exercises and is very popular. In this form, light loads are lifted in quick spurts. The best strength training exercises to use in this form are those that involve weight-lifting. This phase of training generally lasts from four to six weeks, with two sessions per week.

Sample 12-Month Workout Plan

Since football seasons are broken into three phases, it is important to create a custom work out plan that spans a twelve-month timeframe. Remember, the season is broken down into the off-season, in-season and transition periods between the two. The best strategy is to combine a mixture of the different strength training routines you've just read about.

Let's say that your off-season occurs between February and August. You can work on one type of training for the first few months, then start alternating. For example, you can do circuit training for two months and then hypertrophy training for two weeks. The best combination to follow is: circuit training, hypertrophy training, maximal strength training, followed by two weeks of circuit training, one week of maximal strength training and one week of hypertrophy training. Then you can finish the off-season with two weeks of hypertrophy training followed by two weeks of maximal strength training followed by two more weeks of maximal strength training followed by hypertrophy training followed by circuit training and so on until the playing season begins.

Let's say your in-season is between September and December. I would recommend circuit training once a week, combined with either hypertrophy or maximal strength training once a week until the transition period, when you just rest. Your number of sessions per week should greatly reduce during the in-season.

Note that your twelve-month workout program will vary, depending on what position you play and your physical strengths and weaknesses . Knowing what muscles you need to build will enable you to tailor a routine that will work most effectively for you.

Chapter 5: Diet And Nutrition For Athletes

Nutrition is a vital component of athletic performance. Your diet directly affects your performance, so a healthy diet is essential to fuel your training. Understanding the facts of proper diet and nutritional habits is important to achieving a powerful performance. The proper food and water can enhance your strength, stamina, speed, and mental performance.

Not only does maintaining a healthy body boost your physical performance, it also keeps fat away. Excess body fat can drastically decrease your speed, endurance, and agility.

As an athlete, it is best to spend the same amount of effort and attention on your dietary habits that you give to your performance on the field. If you focus more on your performance than your nutrition your body will be imbalanced and will likely perform poorly. Taking care of your body will help prevent injuries and can help you heal faster if you do become injured.

It is important to be aware of when, what, and how much you eat and drink. A healthy diet often requires athletes to exert self-discipline. Each player is different. There is no single "miracle diet" For all athletes. You may find it necessary to periodically adjust your diet, based on your body's needs throughout the year. The key is to find a balance that provides your body with the energy you need for peak performance.

Carbohydrates

Football frequently requires short, intense bursts of energy. Carbohydrates are the most important nutrients for a football player. Including enough of them in your diet can help sustain your body, giving you the stamina to endure to the end of the game and help bring your team to victory.

Eating more carbohydrates translates into having more energy. Sixty percent of your daily calories should consist of "healthy" carbs, carbohydrates with a low fat content. Only thirty percent of your daily calories should come from "healthy" fats. These fats are found in nuts, meats, and dairy products. Even avocados are a great source of healthy fats, while providing additional nutrients.

Avoid foods that contain high amounts of unhealthy fat. This can be easier than it sounds. I recommend asking yourself if there is a healthier alternative to what you're about to eat. For example, a bagel would be a better option than a donut; grilled chicken is a better option than fried chicken. Fried foods can also cause stomach discomfort, further hindering your performance.

Some football players engage in **carbo-loading** a few days before a big competition. Carbo-loading consists of eating massive amounts of carbohydrates while you rest from training. Carbo-loading can build up the levels of glycogen stored in your muscles, which can be released as you move to help energize your body throughout the game.

Protein

Protein is important for building muscle mass. You must carefully track how much protein you consume, because too much of it can lead to dehydration. Only fifteen percent of your daily calories should consist of protein.

While we do not normally consider fruit as a source of protein, a serving of the right kind of fruit can provide up to six percent of your daily protein requirement. The top six protein providers in that category are dried apricots (not fresh), raisins, guavas, dates, prunes, and avocados.

Vegetables can also contribute protein to your diet. Top protein-providers are soybeans, peas, lentils, any type of bean, and spinach.

Fruits and vegetables are great sources of protein and are generally very healthy for your entire body. Most vegetarian dishes contain more than enough protein to meet this requirement.

Recreational football does not provide nearly the nutritional challenges of professional play. While the majority of a game consists of low-intensity movements, a player's increased heart rate and body temperature will consume a great amount of energy. For example, a top-rated professional player would engage in at least 150 small – yet intense – actions throughout a single game.

To ensure that your body can produce enough energy to perform at its best requires a diet that will give your body the simple carbohydrates, protein, healthy fats, and the vitamins and minerals your body needs to stay in tip-top shape. A varied diet can also provide you with benefits in the form of a great-looking and great-feeling body, consistency in performance, and a high level of self-confidence.

Your total energy needs will dictate how much food you is optimum for you. Although there is no formula for the perfect diet, you can formulate yours by considering how much you train, how much you play, whether you are actively playing or in the off-season, what injuries you are dealing with, and your physical size. For example, if you frequently train and play with no complications, your energy needs will be higher than if you're in the off-season or are sitting out due to an injury.

A **pregame meal** is a great strategy to fuel your body for optimum performance. Your pregame meal should consist of low-fat foods. Foods high in fat take longer to digest and can actually sap your playing energy in the process. You can break down your pregame meal into several smaller meals.

Start prepping your body for your big game from the moment you eat breakfast. Breakfast is the foundational meal of your day, so it is important to avoid the mistake of skipping it. Start fueling your body with carbohydrates from common breakfast foods such as toast, cereal, eggs, or steel-cut oats with fresh berries. A smoothie is also an excellent choice.

For lunch and dinner, it is best to consume grilled meats, vegetables, pasta and a fueling beverage such as a sports drink.

Immediately after play has ended, or at least within thirty minutes of stopping, you should consume a **postgame snack** to replenish your fluids, replace your energy stores, and start to heal your muscle tissue. This snack should be a mixture of lean proteins for muscle repair, healthy fats and simple carbohydrates. Examples of a healthy postgame snack include hummus, string cheese, yogurt with fruit, rice cakes, peanut butter and jelly on whole-grain bread, washed down with water.

After your game or workout, you should eat a **postgame meal** to refuel yourself. Some good ideas for a postgame meal include steak, rice, salmon, salads, roast beef, potatoes, and grilled chicken.

Important Tips:

- Watch how much caffeine you consume on a daily basis; it can make you hungrier throughout the day. Following a game, however, a small amount of caffeine can help to increase your blood flow which makes it easier for the needed nutrients to reach and begin to repair damaged tissues.

- Avoid soda. The high sugar content as well as the carbonation in soda can cause your body to work harder than necessary, thus robbing you of energy more profitably burned on the field.

- Avoid fast food and processed foods, which contain chemicals that may work against your body.

- Fresh food is always best. It provides the most nutrients per bite and you avoid unnecessary chemical additives.

Stay Hydrated

Staying hydrated is not just important for playing sports. It is important for everyone, every day. The conditions of the game are your best source of information for determining your hydration needs. Most football games are played outdoors in warm, humid conditions that cause you to sweat and require ongoing rehydration. Games played in cold conditions may not require nearly as much hydration.

If you go too long without drinking liquids, it is possible to become dehydrated. Left untreated, dehydration can lead to cramping, heat exhaustion, brain swelling, seizures, hypovolemic shock (in which your body doesn't have enough blood to circulate around your body), kidney failure, and in extreme cases it may result in coma, stroke or death. To keep adequately hydrated throughout a game or practice, begin by drinking twenty ounces of fluid one to two hours before you start. Drink at least eight more ounces about fifteen minutes before you start. If you're working out, drink eight ounces of fluid every ten minutes.

If you experience a sudden onset of dizziness, vomiting, fatigue, weakness, muscle cramps, or a headache, you should immediately stop whatever you're doing and hydrate yourself. If you stop sweating, this is a major indication that you are seriously dehydrated and need liquids right away.

Vitamins and Minerals

Providing your body with the appropriate amount of vitamins and minerals can help your body function healthily. Most fresh foods contain these elements, which start working upon consumption, but you can also ingest them through supplements. Vitamins and minerals won't boost your energy levels by themselves, but they combine with other substances to facilitate the healthy functioning of your entire body. The better shape your body is in, the easier it can produce energy. Especially important are iron, copper, manganese, magnesium, selenium, sodium, zinc, and vitamins A, C, E, B6, and B12.

Iron

Iron is important for your body, because it helps oxygen travel through your lungs. It also helps your muscles utilize oxygen. Deficiencies in iron can lead to anemia, a condition where your body does not contain enough hemoglobin. Anemia can lead to fatigue. A typical, healthy adult should ingest eight milligrams of iron each day. Good food sources for iron include soybeans, spinach, lentils, chickpeas, liver, lean ground beef, clams, and oysters.

Copper

Copper helps the formation of red blood cells. It can help prevent osteoporosis and can help your heart and arteries function properly. Copper deficiencies can cause chronic diarrhea and fatigue. A typical, healthy adult needs about 900 mcg of copper each day. Shellfish, vegetables, and whole grains can be good natural sources for copper.

Manganese

Manganese is important for your body, because it helps metabolize fats and carbohydrates as well as stimulating the growth of your bones and connective tissues. It can also help protect your body against free radicals and protect against osteoporosis, arthritis, and diabetes. A typical, healthy adult should receive between 1.8 and 2.3 milligrams of manganese each day. The natural sources of manganese include pineapple, nuts, seeds, oats, unrefined cereals, and wheat germ.

Magnesium

Magnesium helps prevent the development of type two diabetes and heart disease. It can help keep your muscles, bones, and nerves strong. Deficiencies in magnesium can lead to irregular heartbeat, irritability, and muscle weakness. A typical, healthy adult should get between 270 and 400 milligrams of magnesium each day. Foods that contain magnesium include whole grains, avocados, nuts, dark greens, and soybeans.

Selenium

Selenium is an antioxidant that can help protect your body against free radicals. It can also help boost your immune system and your thyroid function. It can help protect you from prostate cancer and heart disease. Selenium deficiencies may lead to thyroid problems and heart issues. A typical, healthy adult should get between 55 and 70 mcg of selenium each day. Brazil nuts contain the most concentrated selenium of any food. You can also ingest selenium by eating whole grains, garlic, raisins, walnuts, fish, shellfish, and sunflower seeds.

Sodium

Sodium is important because it helps your body balance its water content and assists in digesting food. It also helps your circulatory and nervous systems function properly. Sodium can help prevent blood clots and high blood pressure. A typical, healthy adult should ingest between 1,500 and 2,000 milligrams of sodium per day. Sodium is naturally found in many foods that are part of a healthy diet.

Zinc

Zinc helps boost your immune system, it can help preserve your vision, and it can stimulate the healing of wounds. Deficiencies in zinc can lead to skin rashes, weight loss, hair loss, and depression. A typical, healthy adult should absorb 15 milligrams of zinc each day. Animal based foods are excellent sources for zinc, as are nuts and some plant-based foods.

Vitamin A

Vitamin A helps your bones grow and helps improve both your immune system and your reproductive health. It can help fend off certain viruses and bacteria and has been known to help improve vision. Deficiencies in vitamin A can lead to night blindness and can turn common ailments like measles or pneumonia into a fatal disease. The best natural source of vitamin A is beef liver. Three ounces of beef liver will provide your body with more than enough of this vitamin for a day. You can also get vitamin A by eating fruits and vegetables.

Vitamin C

To help your body absorb iron, you need Vitamin C. Vitamin C also helps your body repair tissues. It helps protect your body from free radicals and can help your body resist the common cold. Deficiencies in vitamin C can lead to aches in your joints and muscles, muscle weakness, and rashes on your legs. A typical healthy adult male needs around ninety milligrams of vitamin C per day, while a typical female requires about seventy-five milligrams daily. Pregnant women and smokers should consult their doctors about increasing their intake of vitamin C. Vitamin C appears – to varying degrees – in most fruits and vegetables, but its highest concentrations reside in oranges and yellow bell peppers.

Vitamin E

Vitamin E is important for your body because it helps keep your skeletal muscles strong. It is also known to boost your immune system and help form red blood cells. Although vitamin E deficiencies are rare, common signs include slowed healing, leg cramps, and gastrointestinal issues. Healthy adults need about 15 milligrams per day. The best natural sources for vitamin E include spinach, avocados, whole grains, nuts, wheat germ, and vegetable oils.

Vitamin B6

Vitamin B6 is important for your body because it helps your brain communicate with the nerves to regulate your metabolism. It can also boost your immune system. Vitamin B6 can also help prevent or treat carpel tunnel syndrome, depression, asthma attacks, kidney stones, some forms of arthritis, and premenstrual syndrome. Deficiencies in vitamin B6 can cause damage to the nerves in your hands and feet. It can also cause dysplasia in women. A typical, healthy adult requires between 1.3 and 1.7 milligrams of vitamin B6 per day. The best sources for this vitamin include beans, bananas, cheese, milk, vegetables, sunflower seeds, and fish.

Vitamin B12

Vitamin B12 helps your body create red blood cells and it helps maintain your nerve cells. Additionally, it helps create DNA and RNA. Deficiencies of B12 can cause dizziness, fatigue, oral issues, appetite suppression, diarrhea, and muscle weakness. It can also cause you to develop anemia. Vegetarians and vegans tend to have deficiencies in vitamin B12 it is most commonly accessed through animal sources. A typical, healthy adult needs 2.6 mcg of vitamin B12 each day. The best natural sources of B12 include milk, eggs, cheese, fish, poultry, meat, and shellfish.

Antioxidants

Antioxidants help your body protect its tissues against the wear and tear caused by intense exercise. Antioxidants protect your body from free radicals, which damage your muscles through oxidation. Without enough antioxidants in your system, your body will find it difficult to heal your muscles.

A healthy diet usually enables your body's tissues to rebuild naturally. It is important to supply your body with antioxidants via natural sources. Experts have found that ingesting antioxidants in supplement form provides little benefit and excessive supplemental dosages can destroy your body's ability to create its own.

Oxidation can lower your immune system, leaving you susceptible to colds and the flu, either of which may force you to spend time off the field. Spending too much time on the sidelines seems like a waste of all your hard-earned physical conditioning.

The best time to ingest antioxidants is following a workout, a practice, or a competition. Post-activity is the best time to optimize physical recovery. Fruits and vegetables are the leading sources of antioxidants but you can also find them in beans, nuts, dark chocolate, lean meats, seafood, whole grains, and beverages such as green tea and red wine.

Chapter 6: Building Mental Toughness

While physical training and strength are obviously important when it comes to playing football, building your mental strength is equally essential to a well-rounded player. Using sports psychology and specific mental techniques, you can reach your football ambitions more quickly.

Clarify Your Self Image

Employ positive mental images. Envisioning yourself in a positive light will enable you to build your inner strength, increase your emotional power and enhance positive feelings such as motivation and confidence. A healthy self-image can help propel you toward your goals. Visualization can also help boost your physical strength because it releases dopamine and noradrenaline; these hormones help you reach physical peak performance.

The key to successful visualization is to practice it several times a day until it comes naturally. The more of your senses you can activate within your visualization, the stronger will be its affect. Think about what you can see, hear, smell, or touch in addition to what you can see. To me, positive mental images often appear in the form of a vivid daydream. I just sit back, relax, and let my imagination work its muscles and help me envision what I want the most.

Visualize the ball. Yes, you have spent a lot of time on the field playing with the ball and throwing it around, but take a minute to just think about the ball. Imagine that you are watching a video of yourself moving with the ball. Visualize yourself in the third person, as if from a video camera about twenty feet away. Watch yourself executing your favorite moves and performing flawlessly. The more you do this, the better you are likely to perform when a similar situation arises on the playing field.

Before each game or practice, take ten minutes to practice visualizations. This powerful strategy can greatly improve your performance, if implemented consistently. One final tip: whenever you are learning a new technique, repeatedly visualize yourself executing each small detail flawlessly. It may speed your learning process.

Positive affirmations produce powerful results. Everybody thinks negative thoughts. It is human nature. However, consciously making *positive* self-statements can combat them. I highly recommend creating several confidence-building affirmations and repeating them out loud many times a day. After several hundred repetitions, your deepest being will start to believe your statements and your willpower will follow along.

For example, instead of thinking, "Training is tiring me out so badly that I just want to give up!" think, "I easily complete my training exercises." This may sound counter-intuitive and it may not hold true for leaping tall buildings with a single bound, but positive affirmations really do help you keep your focus on – and strengthen your confidence in – your goal.

Choose to be optimistic! Have you ever heard that attitude is everything? People who maintain negative attitudes about life tend to follow them up with actions which yield less-than-stellar consequences. People who sustain an optimistic and positive attitude are more likely to realize their dreams and see success.

By simply choosing a positive outlook on life, your chances of later looking back on a fulfilled life will increase. For example, let's say your friend works a high-paying job while you work for the minimum wage. If you constantly mope about, bemoaning your situation and wallowing over the feeling that your life is less worth living than your friend's, you will be too distracted to look for ways to improve your own paycheck. Studies have shown that optimistic people have a much higher chance of spotting opportunities and capitalizing on them than pessimistic people. It's your choice, but the evidence is clearly in favor of choosing optimism.

Sharpen Your Focus

The 80/20 rule (also known as the pareto principle) points out that you often can isolate the most important twenty percent of what you are doing and discover this is the source of the greatest portion of your success (the eighty percent). While the remaining eighty percent of your efforts are still necessary, it is often possible to make the most of that twenty percent to maximize your success.

For example, if you are able to increase your physical strength most significantly using a small handful of exercises, it makes sense to focus your attention on those exercises. Of course, it is important to continue to work the rest of your muscles, to avoid becoming unbalanced.

Avoid comparisons. It is easy to compare yourself to others and think how poorly you play compared to them. Get those thoughts out of your head right now! Comparison is a distraction. It takes your eyes off of your job and actually prevents you from performing at your best. Learn to accept both your strengths and your weaknesses. Total self-acceptance sets you free to share your teammates' joy in their incredible plays, while allowing you to revel in your own athletic prowess.

Dwell on the Present. Dwelling on the past is easy, but it won't get you anywhere in the present. Neither regret nor resting on your laurels will fuel future success. Only what you think and do in the here and now will shape your future. For example, if you want be a professional player, thinking about your past successes will not propel you there. While past successes and past failures *can* motivate you to work harder and smarter, it's only the training and practice you do *today* that will move you closer to your goal.

Learn to concentrate. During a game, there are all sorts of external distractions. Fans roar, opposing players taunt, and officials make decisions you don't like. You must learn to discard everything that distracts you from the object of the moment and concentrate on the game, your teammates, and your place in it all. Your mind is an amazing instrument, capable of filtering through millions of sensory stimuli and selecting only the information that is needed in a given situation. Trust your mind and help it stay focused.

A pregame ritual can help set up your mind for success in this area. Your ritual may include visualization of yourself successfully negotiating key game scenarios, relaxing – or revving yourself up – with music, reviewing detailed memories of past victories (your personal internal highlights reel), self-coaching, or anything else that will motivate you to get in the "zone."

Break down your goals into smaller steps that are easier to attain. Let's say your primary objective is to be professionally recruited. Of course, there are a host of things that have to happen before you can reach that point. You will need adequate physical stamina, technique, mental strength, a well-developed physique, and strong communication skills. Each of these needs can be separated out into individual goals, some of which can be pursued simultaneously.

You can start by focusing on building your physical stamina and strength. Once you have built enough to increase your activity level, you can maintain these strengths as you shift your focus to building specific playing techniques and increasing your mental toughness. Then pick up the focus on your communication and people skills. When you have reached the point that you're fully prepared to interact with recruiters and the general public, you can continue to cycle your focus between each area until you've successfully reached professional status.

Anticipate Difficulties

Eliminate distractions. Tune out any friends or family members who don't support your endeavors. Surround yourself with people who serve as a strong support system. During training, avoid anything that will tempt you to slack off, things like excessive use of social media, video games, or television viewing. I have known some individuals to put a small padlock through the plug of their electronics and then give the key to a trusted friend until they're ready for time off.

Learn to handle the fear of failure. Fear is an emotion we all experience. However, for athletes, fear can be incredibly debilitating. The fear of failure can either immobilize you or its power can be harnessed and utilized to propel you toward your dreams. The key is to learn how to make your fear work *for* you instead of against you.

When I am preparing for a public speaking event, fear often lurks right behind my shoulder, whispering tales of dire failure into my ear. I can try to ignore it, swatting fear away like a pesky fly as I try to focus on my preparations. If I do this, my fear will ultimately succeed, because it can stick around, preventing me from completely focusing my attention on what I'm doing to get ready for the big day. Then, when the day comes, fear is still clinging to my back, still whispering nasty nothings into my ear, and still preventing me from giving from the best of myself to other people.

However, it is possible to recruit your fear to serve you. This occurs not by avoiding or ignoring fear, but by turning to face it and daring it to do its worst. Stop what you're doing at the moment and give your full attention to what fear is saying. Ignore how it makes you feel and focus on the "facts" behind your fear. What is the absolute worst that can happen? Imagine that very scenario happening to you, then imagine yourself recovering and moving forward to the next thing. Did you notice? The thing you feared most did not kill you. Embarrassment, yes. Humiliation, probably. Pain, possibly. But you emerged on the other side, alive. Fear couldn't touch what makes you *you*. If that's the worst you will suffer at the hands of fear, then why worry?

Every time fear rears its ugly head, give it a good hard stare and remind it that fear has no authority over your life. Then turn your face forward and use the emotional energy that was stirred up as impetus to spur yourself forward in determination to reach your goal.

Learn to handle rejection. Like fear, rejection is something we all face. In the same way that you face your fears head-on, you can gain strength from others' rejection. Instead of viewing rejection as an indication that you are a failure, look at it as one step in the elimination process. So, you aren't wanted by the Vikings right now; you've just eliminated one option on the way to discovering where you *are* wanted.

Yes, rejection hurts; it means the death of a dream (or one path to your dream) and as such, you are right to grieve the loss. Allow yourself to experience grief, but don't let yourself be deceived into thinking there are no more dreams to be had. There is a time to let go of grief in order to grasp life's next opportunity.

If you are fortunate enough to learn *why* you were rejected, you have just been handed a gift. Extract all the potential goodness from that criticism; look for ways you can increase your communication skills, strengthen your physical skills, or otherwise present yourself more accurately in the future.

Fortunately, your critics are not the final judge of your life. Often, criticism is offered from a genuine desire to see you grow. Even if it is not, there is always a kernel of truth you can pull out of the criticism; use it to build yourself into an even more powerful person. If you can receive criticism and rejection without blowing your lid, you will be much better off in your journey through life.

Beat Performance Anxiety. Some athletes find themselves nervous before a big game, even if they are star players. This is common. Performance anxiety preys on areas in which you lack confidence; without proper management, it can put a crimp in your performance, no matter how skilled you are. It can manifest physically as tight muscles, difficulty breathing, upset stomach, or an elevated heart rate. Mentally, anxiety can wreak havoc on your focus and concentration.

To beat performance anxiety, you must be self-aware of and adopt a positive attitude toward your feelings. Instead of letting your anxiety scare you, look at it as a side-effect of gearing up for the game. When you start to feel anxious, tell your jitters, "Let's go out there and play!" Once you're on the field, your jitters will go away, leaving you with the spurt of energy you need to dive into the game. Mastering pre-game jitters is one aspect of mental toughness.

While it is easy to focus on things that are out of your control, such as losing a game or being unable to train due to an injury, the best strategy is to focus on what you **can** control, which is mainly your attitude. A positive attitude cannot change the present but it can help make the situation easier to live through.

Behave professionally. This is another indicator of mental toughness. It is not uncommon for athletes to get caught up in a frustrating moment and "blow off steam" in the form of yelling, throwing things, or otherwise acting out. Many people view this as typical behavior that helps athletes refocus. However, that kind of behavior is unprofessional. It shines a negative light on the whole team, and it sends an unhealthy message to all the kids out there who are modeling your behavior.

Research shows that players perform best when they feel calm, even athletes who are infamous for emotional outbursts such as Tiger Woods. Instead of exploding, take deep a few slow, deep breaths, then focus on what you can learn from the situation. A player might say "Okay, so I fumbled the ball. Now I know to open my hands wider next time. Time to let it go and move on."

Believe in yourself! One of the biggest hindrances to success is self-doubt. It will be difficult to reach success if you cannot realistically see yourself living in success. If you think you are not as good as everyone else, if you feel you are not worthy of success, or if you fear that you just do not have what it takes, you are setting yourself up for failure. On the other hand, with enough practice, hard work, and a bit of confidence, you can do anything you see others doing.

Have faith in yourself and you will be amazed at how far you can go. Sometimes all it takes to be a successful person is to sustain both a strong desire and a good work ethic. If you do something enough times you are bound to become an expert, eventually. As long as you don't give up, you are still on the road to success.

Conclusion

I hope this book was able to help you to understand what it takes to become a successful football player.

Your next step is to start developing habits based on your personal needs. Start by ensuring that you have the proper equipment and that you understand how to play the game. Then develop a good stretching and warm-up routine to reduce your chances of injury on the field. Depending on your experience in the game and what position you play, you should select and implement a few of the strategies we discussed in Chapter Three. Keep practicing these strategies until you have mastered them, then begin gradually to add in others that will help you become a well-rounded player. Analyze your diet and see what you can do differently to provide your body with adequate energy and the power necessary to play and train. Then plan out your twelve-month strength training program to top it all off!

Finally, if you discovered at least one thing that has helped you or that you think would be beneficial to someone else, be sure to take a few seconds to easily post a quick positive review. As an author, your positive feedback is desperately needed. Your highly valuable five star reviews are like a river of golden joy flowing through a sunny forest of mighty trees and beautiful flowers! *To do your good deed in making the world a better place by helping others with your valuable insight, just leave a nice review.*

My Other Books and Audio Books
www.AcesEbooks.com

Health Books

ULTIMATE HEALTH SECRETS

HEALTH

Strategies For Dieting, Eating Healthy, Exercising, Losing Weight, The Mediterranean Diet, Strength Training, And All About Vitamins, Minerals, And Supplements

Ace McCloud

ENERGY
ULTIMATE ENERGY

Discover How To Increase Your Energy Levels Using The Best All Natural Foods, Supplements And Strategies For A Life Full Of Abundant Energy

Ace McCloud

RECIPE BOOK

The Best Food Recipes That Are Delicious, Healthy, Great For Energy And Easy To Make

Ace McCloud

MASSAGE THERAPY

TRIGGER POINT THERAPY
ACUPRESSURE THERAPY
Learn The Best Techniques For Optimum Pain Relief And Relaxation

Ace McCloud

LOSE WEIGHT

THE TOP 100 BEST WAYS TO LOSE WEIGHT QUICKLY AND HEALTHILY

Ace McCloud

FATIGUE
OVERCOME CHRONIC FATIGUE

Discover How To Energize Your Body & Mind So That You Can Bring The Energy & Passion Back Into Your Life

Ace McCloud

Peak Performance Books

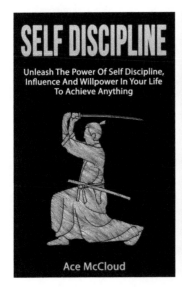

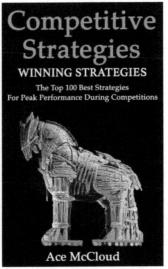

Be sure to check out my audio books as well!

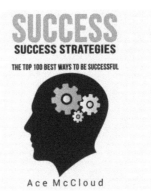

Check out my website at: **www.AcesEbooks.com** for a complete list of all of my books and high quality audio books. I enjoy bringing you the best knowledge in the world and wish you the best in using this information to make your journey through life better and more enjoyable! **Best of luck to you!**

CPSIA information can be obtained
at www.ICGtesting.com
Printed in the USA
BVHW07s2133140818
524469BV00005B/143/P

9 781640 480278